Edited by JANE YOLEN

With musical arrangements by ADAM STEMPLE

Pictures by CHARLES MIKOLAYCAK

THE LULLABY SONGBOOK

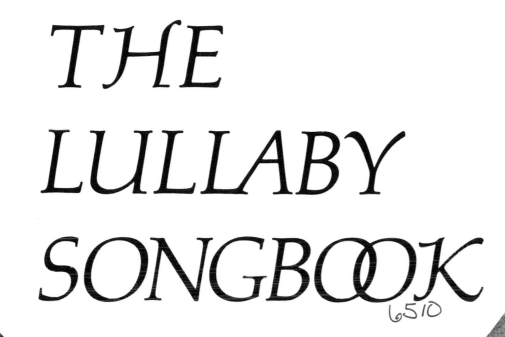

HBJ

Harcourt Brace Jovanovich, Publishers
San Diego   New York   London

"All Through the Night," words© J. B. Cramer & Co. Ltd. Used by permission.

Library of Congress Cataloging-in-Publication Data
Main entry under title:
The Lullaby songbook.
   For piano; with interlinear words.
   Includes chord symbols.
   Summary: A collection of fifteen lullabies, each
with a historic note and a musical arrangement.
   1. Lullabies. [1. Lullabies. 2. Songs]
I. Yolen, Jane. II. Stemple, Adam. III. Mikolaycak,
Charles, ill.
M1997.L95 1986   85-752855
ISBN 0-15-249903-2

Printed in the United States of America

First edition

A B C D E

The paintings in this book were done by applying watercolors and colored
   pencils to Diazo prints made from the original pencil drawings.
The text type was set in Paladium by Hillcrest Graphics, San Diego, California.
The display type was set in Palatino Italic by Thompson Type, San Diego,
   California.
Color separations were made by Heinz Weber, Inc., Los Angeles, California.
Printed by Holyoke Lithograph Company, Springfield, Massachusetts.
Bound by The Book Press, Brattleboro, Vermont.
Production supervision by Warren Wallerstein.
Designed by Dalia Hartman.

With love to John Gregory Yolen and
with thanks to Joyce Rankin

—J. Y. and A. S.

Special thanks to Kathy, Lisa, and Dalia

—C. M.

TABLE OF CONTENTS

SLEEP, BABY, SLEEP

Though this lullaby found its way into early
collections in English as early as the 18th century,
it is really a translation from an older German song,
"Schlaf, Kindlein, Schlaf."

ALL THROUGH THE NIGHT

The people of Wales have a long tradition of group singing and one of their most popular songs is this lullaby, called in Welsh *Ar Hyd Y Nos*. The words by Sir Harold Boulton, written in 1884, were set to a much older melody.

H. Boulton

Tune traditional

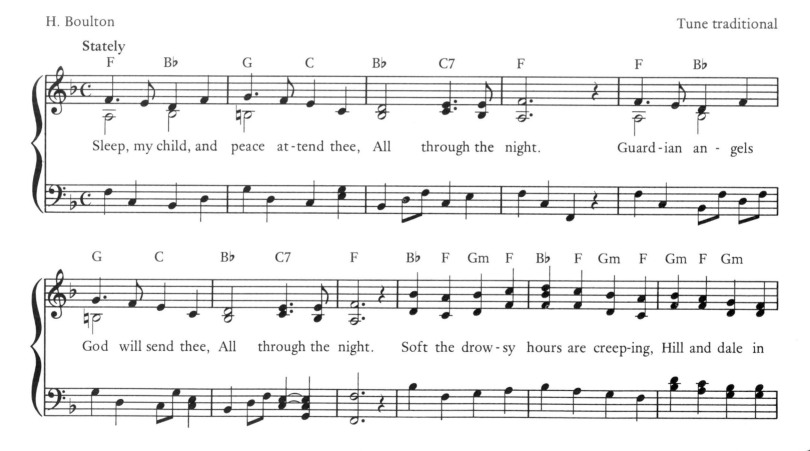

Sleep, my child, and peace at-tend thee, All through the night. Guard-ian an - gels

God will send thee, All through the night. Soft the drow-sy hours are creep-ing, Hill and dale in

8

slum - ber steep - ing. I my lov - ing vig - il keep - ing, All through the night.

2.
While the moon her watch is keeping,
All through the night,
While the weary world is sleeping
All through the night,
O'er thy spirit gently stealing,
Visions of delight revealing,
Breathes a pure and holy feeling,
All through the night.

HUSH, LITTLE BABY

A Southern Appalachian play-party song, this was
also sung for years as a lullaby. The English tradition
it stems from is much older than its Southern
incarnation.

Traditional

Chirrupy

Hush, lit-tle ba-by, don't say a word, Pa-pa's going to buy you a mock-ing-bird. And

if that mock-ing - bird don't sing, Pa-pa's going to buy you a dia-mond ring.

10

2.
If that diamond ring turns brass,
Papa's going to buy you a looking glass.
And if that looking glass gets broke,
Papa's going to buy you a billy goat.

3.
And if that billy goat won't pull,
Papa's going to buy you a cart and bull.
And if that cart and bull turns over,
Papa's going to buy you a dog named Rover.

4.
If that dog named Rover don't bark,
Papa's going to buy you a horse and cart.
And if that horse and cart falls down,
You'll still be the sweetest little baby in town.

LULLOO LULLAY

This lullaby was first published as a poem in the storybook *Gwinellen, the Princess Who Could Not Sleep* (Macmillan, 1964).

J. Yolen

Dolefully

Lul - loo lul - lay, by night and day, The hood - ed hours ride by. _____ And

no one knows just where time goes, Un - til he closes his eyes. _____ So

BY'M BYE

Part of an old black spiritual, this fragment took
on its own life as a lullaby and is now more popular
than the spiritual ever was.

BYE BABY BUNTING

The word *bunting* in this most popular of English lullabies is an old term of endearment meaning "short and thick . . . as a plump child." The skin used to wrap the baby in has been variously called "hare skin," "lamb skin," "bullie's skin," or for the more adventurous daddy, "a sturdy lion's skin."

Traditional

With a little bounce

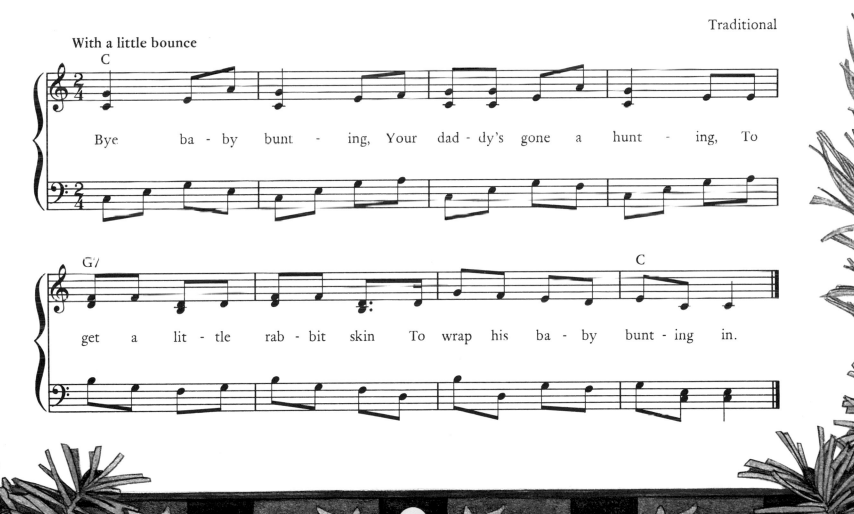

Bye ba - by bunt - ing, Your dad - dy's gone a hunt - ing, To

get a lit - tle rab - bit skin To wrap his ba - by bunt - ing in.

RAISINS AND ALMONDS

This Yiddish cradle song was popularized in America by folksingers in the 1950s and 1960s, and though its origins are far older, it has remained a standard lullaby since that time.

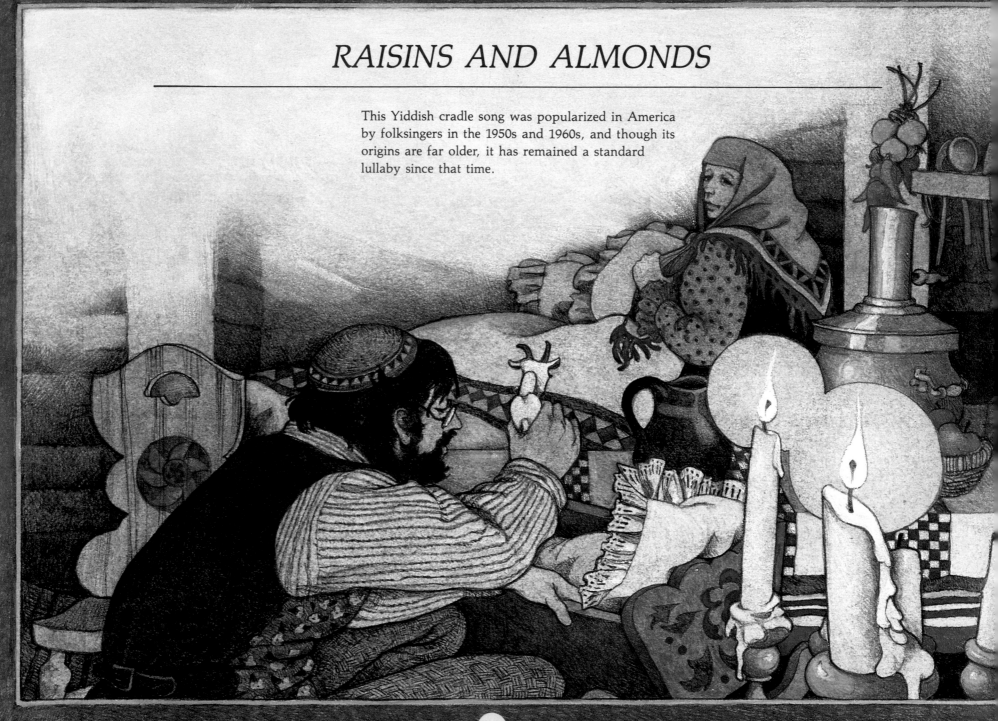

ALL THE PRETTY LITTLE HORSES

A deceptive lullaby out of the American south, this
is as much protest as prayer. Tradition has it that
the song was sung by a black woman rocking her
master's child while her own babe lay unattended.

Traditional

With gentle sadness

Hush - a - by, Don't you cry, Go to sleep - y, lit - tle ba - by.

When you wake, You shall have All the pret - ty lit - tle hors - es.

Blacks and bays, Dap-ples and grays, Coach and six___ lit-tle hors - es.

2.
Down in the meadow
Lies a poor little lambie.
Bees and butterflies
Pickin' on its eyes,
Poor little thing is cryin' Mammy.
Blacks and bays,
Dapples and grays,
Coach and six little horses.

BALOO BALEERIE

This Gaelic lullaby celebrates the small inner room,
the "ben," or nursery where the baby sleeps.

Traditional

Ba - loo ba - lee - rie, ba - loo ba - lee - rie, ba - loo ba -

lee - rie, Ba - loo ba - lee. Go a - way, lit - tle fair - ies, Go a -

way,   lit - tle fair – ies, Go a - way,   lit - tle fair – ies, From our   small room.

(As it is sung in Scotland)

Gang awa' peerie fairies,	Doun come the bonny angels,	Sleep saft my baby,
Gang awa' peerie fairies,	Doun come the bonny angels,	Sleep saft my baby,
Gang awa' peerie fairies	Doun come the bonny angels,	Sleep saft my baby,
Frae oor ben noo.	Tae oor ben noo.	In oor ben noo.

CUM BY YAH

This traditional black spiritual was originally called "Come By Here, Lord." When it was exported along the trade-and-slave routes backward to the West Indies, it became a Pidgin-English lullaby. It then returned to the American continent, where it has been sung by mothers of all races and religions.

Traditional

Rocking

Cum by yah, my Lord, Cum by yah. Cum by yah, my Lord, Cum by yah. Cum by

yah, my Lord, Cum by yah. Yah—yah, Cum by yah. Yah—yah, Cum by yah.——

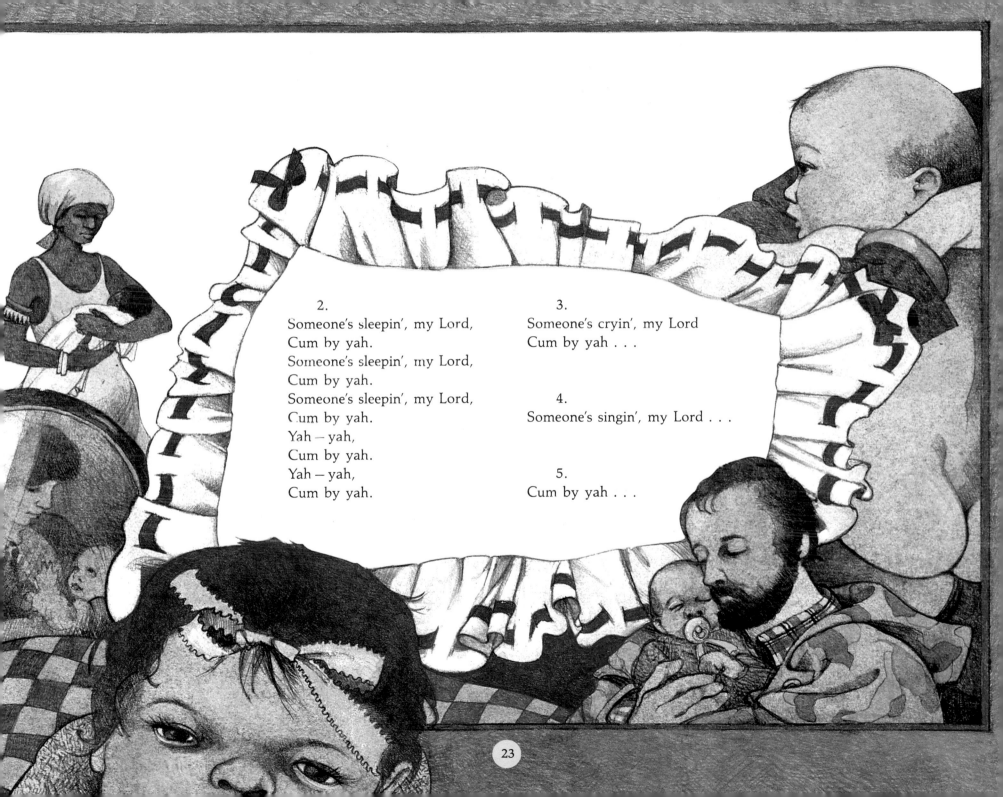

2.
Someone's sleepin', my Lord,
Cum by yah.
Someone's sleepin', my Lord,
Cum by yah.
Someone's sleepin', my Lord,
Cum by yah.
Yah — yah,
Cum by yah.
Yah — yah,
Cum by yah.

3.
Someone's cryin', my Lord
Cum by yah . . .

4.
Someone's singin', my Lord . . .

5.
Cum by yah . . .

SUO GAN

This Irish lullaby found its way into a song collection
in the early 1800s. Folk song scholar Robert Bryan
collected this version, which is now considered
the standard.

Traditional

Sleep, my ba - by, on my bos - om, Warm and coz - y it will prove;

Round thee moth - er's arms are fold - ing, In her heart a moth - er's love.

24

There shall no one come to harm thee, Naught shall ev - er break thy rest.

Sleep my dar - ling babe in qui - et, Sleep on moth - er's gen - tle__ breast.

DANCE TO YOUR DADDY

Up and down the Eastern seacoast of America
fishermen sang this spirited little lullaby to
their children.

Traditional

Gentle spirit

Dance to your dad - dy, my lit - tle ba - by,

Dance to your dad - dy, my lit - tle lamb. You shall have a fish and

you shall have a fin, And you shall have a had-dock when the boat comes in.

2.
Dance to your daddy, my little laddie,
Dance to your daddy, my little man.
You shall have a fishy in a little dishy,
You shall have a fishy when the boat comes in.

ROCK-A-BYE BABY

Also known as "Hush-A-Bye Baby," this song has been called the best known lullaby in English. There is a tradition that it was written by a young *Mayflower* pilgrim after he watched the Indian women rock their children in birchbark cradle boards hung in trees. The song has been found in printed versions as far back as the 18th century.

Traditional

With a rocking manner

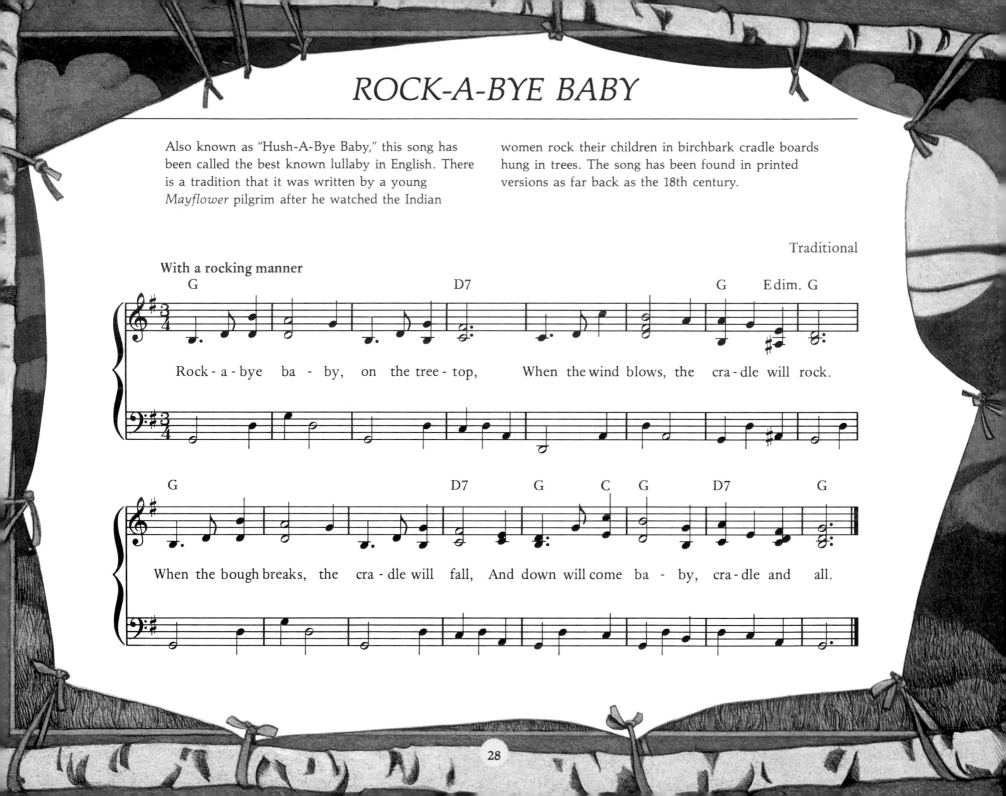

Rock - a - bye ba - by, on the tree - top, When the wind blows, the cra - dle will rock.

When the bough breaks, the cra - dle will fall, And down will come ba - by, cra - dle and all.

NOW THE DAY IS OVER

An old hymn written by Sabine Baring-Gould and set to music by Joseph Barnaby, this song has been used more often as a lullaby than in church.

Baring-Gould

J. Barnaby

In a stately manner

| G | D | G | Em | B7 | Em | Em7 |

Now the day is__ o - ver. Night is draw-ing__ nigh;__

| A7 | | D | G | D7 | | G |

Shad - ows of the eve - ning Steal a - cross the sky.

BRAHMS' LULLABY

This song is known variously as "Lullaby and Goodnight" and "Brahms' Lullaby" after the composer, Johannes Brahms, who wrote it. Brahms' friend and publisher Fritz Simrock wrote the lyrics in German. This translation is one of several that have become popular since 1868, when the song came to America.

Brahms

Lull - a - by,   and good night,   With_ ro - ses be - dight,__ With_ lil - ies be -

decked   Is__ ba - by's wee bed.   Lay thee down   now and rest,   may your slum - ber be

blest.__ Lay thee down   now and rest,   may your slum - ber be   blest.

TO THOSE WHO USE THIS BOOK

One of the tenderest moments an adult and child can share is a lullaby. When my three children were infants, I held them and rocked them to sleep with the songs in this book. It was a comfort to both child and adult. Later, each toddler insisted on a night song as part of his or her bedtime routine. I even sang medleys of lullabies and other quiet songs to the family when we went camping, to bring the comfort of home to the tent, to add a familiar note to the chorus of night creatures who sang their strange lullabies outside.

A crying child could be a danger for a nomadic tribe. Soothing nonsense syllables were the earliest lullabies. *Loo-loo, la-la, lullay, ni-ni, na-na* were the kinds of babbling that became incorporated into songs and, in fact, remain as nonsense refrains in many lullabies. In Italian and Rumanian, the word for rocking a baby to sleep is *ninna-nanna*. The Greek word for lullaby is *nannarismata*. Other names for lullabies, less onomatopoetic, include cradle song, lap song, the French *berceuse*, and the German *wiegenlied*.

In some lullabies, there are praises for the child. In some, promises — horses, dolls, birds to be gotten. In some, the mother complains. And in some, there are threats of the bogeyman, called El Coco or Hotei or the beastly Bonaparte. As a child in summer camp, I learned a particularly gruesome South African lullaby:

> *Siembamba*
> *Mother's baby*
> *Siembamba*
> *Mother's baby.*
> *Twist his neck and hit him in the head.*
> *Roll him in the ditch and he'll be dead.*
> *Siembamba.*

You will not find "Siembamba" or other such lullabies here. I have collected my favorites, the soothing kind, for this book. These are the songs that say to the listening child: *Go to sleep now. I am here. There is nothing you should fear. Sleep. Sleep. Sleep.*

Jane Yolen
Phoenix Farm
Hatfield, Massachusetts